ANIMALS EXPOSED!
The Truth About
Animal Senses

Created and produced by Firecrest Books Ltd
in association with the
John Francis Studio/Bernard Thornton Artists

Copyright © 2002 Firecrest Books Ltd and
John Francis/Bernard Thornton Artists

Published by Tangerine Press,
an imprint of Scholastic Inc;
557 Broadway, New York, NY 10012

Tangerine Press and associated logo and design
are trademarks of Scholastic Inc.

ISBN 0-439-51807-5

Printed and bound in Thailand
First Printing December 2002

ANIMALS EXPOSED!

The Truth About
Animal Senses

Bernard Stonehouse
and Esther Bertram

Illustrated by
John Francis

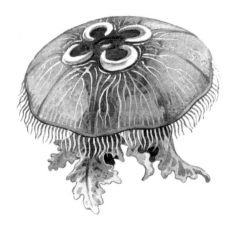

Tangerine Press and associated logo
and design are trademarks of Scholastic Inc.

FOR RACHEL

Art and Editorial Direction by
Peter Sackett and Dr Bob Close

Edited by
Norman Barrett

Designed by
Paul Richards, Designers & Partners

Color separation by
**SC (Sang Choy) International Pte Ltd
Singapore**

Printed and bound by
Sirivatana Interprint Public Co., Ltd., Thailand

Contents

Introduction

What do animals see? What do they hear? What do they feel? Senses are an animal's means of discovering the world around it. Every animal has sense organs, some simple, some very complex, enabling them to see things, hear things, smell, taste, and touch things. These sensations tell them what is happening close by and far away, and help them find their way around.

So do animals see and feel things much as we do? Storytellers relate tales of sneaky squirrels, wise old bears, cunning cats, and faithful dogs. These are fun stories, but don't believe a word of them. Animals are not people – in many ways they can be much more interesting than the people around on your street. Though an animal's eyes, ears, and nose may look much like our own, what it sees, hears, and smells may be very different. Because its brain is different, what it feels is different.

So do animals have feelings? Of course they have feelings, and the fact that they are different can never be an excuse for mistreating them. The more we know about how animals understand, the more marvelous they seem, and the more they earn our respect.

We can start by sorting out truth from myth in the stories about them. Are bats really blind? Do animals with big ears hear better than those with smaller ones? Can hawks see for miles and miles? Do red rags enrage bulls? Do chameleons change color? Can cats see in the dark? Are eight eyes better than two? Look for the answers in the following pages.

Do animals with big ears have better hearing than those with small ones? See pages 20-21.

Simple sight

Single-cell life

Hundreds of different kinds of plants and animals are made up of single cells. They have no eyes, for even the simplest eyes are made up of several dozen cells. Yet many single-cell plants and animals are sensitive to light – enough to move toward dim lights that help them work properly, and away from brighter ones that might harm them.

Do animals see what we see? Some certainly do not. With others we can never be sure. We can only examine them closely, watch their behavior, and try to figure out how much they rely on sight.

This earthworm spends its life burrowing in soil, pushing aside the grains with its pointed front end, making a tube for its body to slither through. It has no eyes and lives mostly in darkness. It eats soil, digesting the tiny animals and plants that grow in it, and expelling the hard grains as worm casts. Worms mostly come out at night, when the air is cooler and there are not so many birds around that might eat them. Shine a flashlight on an earthworm in the dark, and it will withdraw into its burrow. Without eyes, it can still tell light from darkness through its skin. Other animals on these pages get by with no eyes or with very simple eyes.

Floating blind?

A Portuguese man of war is a complicated kind of jellyfish, up to 1 foot (30 cm) across, with long trailing tentacles. It floats on the sea surface, driven by the wind. The tentacles catch small shrimps and draw them into its mouth. Can it see where it's going? Not so far as we know.

Do mussels need eyes?

You wouldn't think so. They live attached to rocks, feeding by drawing sea water through their gills. Yet tiny eye spots along the edges of their open shells are just sensitive enough to detect shadows or slight movements – warnings that hungry birds or fish may be around.

Flatworms

These very simple animals live in the sea, in fresh water, or in damp soils. They have two light-sensitive eyes on the upper surface of their body that, together with other sensory organs, enable them to swim, crawl, and hunt live prey.

Below: An earthworm has no eyes, but can detect light or darkness through its skin.

The eyes have it

Opposite page: Wolf spiders are active hunters that pounce on their prey. Why eight eyes? We do not know, but they are all much simpler and less efficient than ours.

Two eyes, but ...
Squid are sea mollusks – related to snails, cuttlefish, and octopus – that swim fast and use their tentacles to catch prey. Most are less than 2 feet (60 cm) long. Their two big eyes look much like our own, but are made to a simpler pattern and are probably not as effective as ours. Still, they work well enough to make the squid a very efficient hunter.

Squid eyes look like ours but differ inside.

Most animals have two eyes. Are two eyes always better than one? If we damage one of our eyes, we can usually get by with the other. However, having two eyes also allows us to see more of the world, and sometimes to see things more clearly or judge distances better.

This wolf spider has eight eyes. Is this better than two? We are not sure what they are all for, but the spider probably sees most of the world through the two big ones. The smaller ones on top of the head may help it to see all around, the four little ones in front could be to detect movement – all things we can do by turning our head. The squid has two eyes that look very much like ours, but are different inside. The beetle and crab each have two eyes, but each eye is made up of dozens of little ones. The vervet monkey has two eyes that are much like our own.

What a beetle sees
This great diving beetle has just two eyes, but look closely and you'll see that each eye has a honeycomb surface pattern. Each cell of the honeycomb is a separate eye, pointing in a slightly different direction than its neighbors. Many insects have "compound eyes" like these. They provide good all-around vision and help detect movement, without seeing very clearly in any one direction.

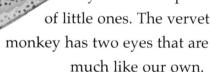

Eyes like ours
Vervet monkeys use their two eyes as we do, to see both distance and close-up. The eyes look forward, allowing the monkey to examine fruit and other objects very close in its hands. Unlike other animals on this page, the monkey can turn its head to look to either the side or behind.

Eyes on stalks
Crabs also have two compound eyes, though simpler and with fewer cells than those of the diving beetle (above). This sandcrab's eyes fold away into grooves when the crab digs into the sand. They unfold and are raised on stalks when it wants to see the world.

Long distance vision

Scent on the wind
Caribou herds in summer graze over enormous areas of Arctic tundra. Camouflaged against the background, they are hard to see at a distance. This wolf picked up the scent of a small herd and tracked it for miles. Now he is watching the herd, and will lead his pack to catch one or more of them.

Looking a long way
Cheetahs on the look-out for food find a rock or tree to climb up to see above the long grass. This female cheetah has spotted a herd of impalas grazing from over a mile (nearly 2 km) away. She and her cubs will make their way over to them, and try to separate one of the calves from the herd.

People who can see things clearly a long way away we call "hawk-eyed." Do hawks see better than other animals? Hawks and other predatory birds with large, forward-looking eyes probably see a broad picture of the countryside, much like we do. However, they are much better than we are at spotting tiny movements at a distance. This male goshawk has seen a movement in the grass 200 feet (60 m) away – a tiny movement that even the sharpest-sighted human would need binoculars to see. It may be a mouse, a vole, even a beetle. Whatever it is, it could mean breakfast for the goshawk and his chicks. Keeping the point of movement in sight, he will glide toward it, hover for a moment, then swoop in and grab it with his sharp claws.

Many other predatory birds and mammals have this kind of vision. Owls use it in dim evening and early-morning light, helped by very sharp hearing. Vultures can spot their prey many miles away, possibly helped by a sense of smell. Cheetahs, wolves, and other mammals that hunt by day also have good long-distance vision.

Seeing and smelling
Vultures soar on updrafts of warm air to heights of 650-1,000 feet (200-300 m). From these heights they can see far across the plains. They can spot where lions and other predators have killed prey, and then descend to feed on the remains. They may be helped in their search by a sharp sense of smell.

Seeing and hearing
Barn owls spend most of their day asleep. They become active in the evening, when the light fades and mice and other small mammals are venturing out to feed. Very acute hearing, as well as sharp eyesight, help them find prey in the dim light.

The sharp-eyed goshawk has detected a slight movement on the ground far below.

Each of these robins, fighting to keep the other out of its territory, is responding mainly to its rival's red face and breast.

Seeing in color

Black and white

To human eyes, this pheasant is brilliantly colored. The dog sees little color, and may find it hard to spot the bird against its green and brown background. He'll know it is there mainly from its scent, which we could not smell at all.

Humans see the world in all the colors of the rainbow, from red through orange, yellow, green, and blue to indigo and violet. This is because we have cells (called cone cells) in the retina at the back of our eyes that are sensitive to colors. But do animals have these color-sensitive cells or do they see only in black and white?

Some kinds of animals see the colors that we see. Most birds see colors much as we do, but reptiles and mammals tend to be colorblind. Birds themselves are often colorful, and use colors to identify themselves to each other. These two male robins are squaring off for a fight. Coming up to breeding time, each sees the other's red breast as a sign of a rival, so they will fight until one or other flies away. It is the color that matters – a robin will fight a bunch of red feathers placed in its territory, but ignore a model robin painted black or green. Bulls, dogs, and most other mammals probably do not see colors at all. Bees and other insects may see colors that we cannot see.

The dog will see the pheasant's movements, but its bright colors will appear in black, white, and shades of gray.

What does a bee see?

Scientists studying bees have found that they respond to colors, but not as we do. Flowers we see as red, they see as black or dark gray. Some that look green to us, they see as brilliant white, and some that are white to us are blue or blue-green to them. Bees can see ultraviolet light and find their way home using polarized light, which we cannot see.

Red rag to a bull?

People say that bulls become angry and dangerous if they see red clothing. Bulls – like dogs – see little difference in colors. But those that are protecting cows during the mating season want to keep any intruders away the woman in green just as much as the man in red.

Sight for survival

Looking far and wide

Compared with monkeys or ourselves, horses, zebras, and many other grazing and browsing animals have eyes that are set apart on a broad skull. This gives them a wide field of vision. Even while grazing, they can keep a sharp lookout for predators, both forward and sideways at the same time, without having to turn their heads.

Do some animals have the ability to spot danger from more than one direction? It pays for animals to be able to see as much as possible of their surroundings, either to hunt as effectively as possible or to make sure that they stay away from danger.

Different animals use their eyes in different ways. Sharks, which are very active hunters, have large eyes and good eyesight. Hammerhead sharks (opposite page) have enormously broad skulls, with their eyes out on the edges, to get a better view of the world.

Wild horses graze on open grassy plains, where they are open to attack from wolves and other predators. Even when they are grazing with head down, their eyes keep a lookout both sideways and forward. Both cod and crabs live mainly on the sea floor, where the biggest dangers come from above. Cod eyes look sideways, crab eyes forward, and both look upward. Dragonflies swooping above ponds and streams need good all-around vision, provided by those huge compound eyes.

Sally-go-lightly crab

Crabs that live on the sea shore and in shallow waters, like this sally-go-lightly crab, have stalked, compound eyes that give them good vision. Despite their small size, they can recognize predatory birds as far away as 50 feet (15 m) and scuttle for safety.

All-seeing hunter

The dragonfly's huge compound eyes, taking up much of its head (below), are made up of thousands of light-sensitive cells pointing forward, upward, and sideways. As a result, dragonflies can see both predators and prey, as well as potential mates, coming from almost any direction.

Danger from above

Like many other deep-water fish, cod have large, flat eyes set on the sides of their head. Large eyes are good for catching the small amount of light that penetrates into deep water. Sideways-looking eyes give them a wide field of vision on either side. They cannot see the seabed immediately below them, but they can tilt their eyes to look upward, which is where attacks from seals, whales, and bigger fish are likely to come.

Opposite page: The hammerhead shark is a dangerous predator, with its good eyesight and wide field of vision on both sides.

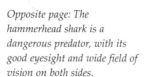

Night vision

Deep-diving seals

Deep-diving seals, such as the elephant seal (below), feed on larger fish and squid in deeper water than most other seals. For this purpose, they have much larger eyes, which let in more light, so they can detect their prey in the murky ocean depths.

This tomcat is hunting by moonlight. But can cats see in the dark? Those big green eyes are wide open, and so are the black pupils. The cat has more rod cells – the kind that are right for night vision – at the back of its eye than we have. So it makes use of every bit of light there is, and sees far more on a dark night than we can. It's using its ears and whiskers, too, to detect movement. On a really dark night, with no moon or starlight, it would find hunting much harder, and probably stay curled up at home. In a really dark room, with no light at all, it would see nothing.

Owls, deep-water fish, bush babies, and some seals also have big eyes and good night vision for hunting in the dark.

A night hunter

Owls hunt mostly at night. Like cats, they have large eyes, with pupils that enlarge to let more light in. Like cats, too, they have sharp hearing. Watching and listening from a tree branch, they can spot a mouse 65 feet (20 m) away and swoop down to catch it.

Deep-water fish

Predatory fish that live in very deep seas often have large eyes. Below about 1,000 feet (300 m) there is no light from the sun or sky. Many of the small fish and shrimp that live down there carry lights to attract each other.

Left: A tomcat on the prowl at night – it has better night vision than we do, but cannot see at all when it is completely dark.

Expanding pupils

Small mammals of the African forest with huge brown eyes, bush babies are night hunters of insects, lizards, and small mammals. The pupils, small black dots in daylight, expand enormously at night to take in every last bit of light, and those large ears twitch and turn to every tiny sound.

Sensing sound

Left: The fennec directs its ears toward the sound coming from under a bush and is ready to pounce.

Keeping cool

With the biggest ears of any animal, should elephants hear best of all? Like the fennec, they hear well and turn their ears to locate sounds. But they use their ears for cooling down. By flapping its big ears, the elephant can keep cool on a hot day.

Life underground

Living underground in tight-fitting tunnels, moles are better off without external ears. They still have ears inside their head, sharp enough to hear each other squeaking and scratching, both in their burrows and at the surface of the ground. They may feel vibrations, too, through their nose and skin.

Sounds are vibrations, or waves, that travel through air, water, or solid materials. Ears are special organs for picking up these vibrations. The external ears, or ear flaps, catch the vibrations. The internal ears are the parts you hear with, tucked away inside your skull. So, the bigger the ear flaps, the better an animal hears – is that true? This fennec, a kind of desert fox, has big ears, but, more importantly, it can turn and twist them toward a source of sound. Out hunting, it has heard a mouse squeaking under a bush, and has turned its ears to locate the sound exactly. That way, it can work out where the mouse is, and pounce on it. Elephants, which have the biggest ears of any land animal, use them for something else as well as hearing.

Moles have hardly any external ears, but can still hear each other squeaking. Fish and snakes, with no external ears, hear vibrations in completely different ways. Big external ears help some animals locate sounds better. Others hear perfectly well with very small ear flaps or

Picking up vibrations

Some animals that live close to the ground "hear" mainly through their bodies. Like other reptiles, this snake has no external ears, and hears very little through the air. But it is very sensitive to vibrations through the ground – enough to keep out of the way when big animals are walking nearby.

Hearing underwater

Can my pet fish hear me? Fish have no external ear flaps, but are very sensitive to vibrations in the water. Many, like this carp, have lines of ear-like organs along both sides of their face and body. Through these they feel and locate disturbances from a long way away.

Interpreting sounds

Opposite page: Birds, like this eastern bluebird, sing to define their territory or to attract mates.

Sounds come in different wavelengths and frequencies. Short waves at high frequencies give us high notes, long waves at lower frequencies give us low notes. Most sounds are mixtures of frequencies, which our ears sort out, helping us recognize musical notes, words, bird songs, and just plain noises. Many animals communicate with each other by sounds. Cats squeal, dogs growl or bark, and this eastern bluebird is singing to tell other birds to keep out of its territory.

Only humans communicate by words. Do animals understand when we speak to them? Intelligent dogs come to recognize "food" and "walk." Cats, horses, and apes, too, pick up individual words and respond to the tone of our voice. But they have no spoken language of their own, and do not understand ours. Some birds – particularly parrots, mynahs, and starlings – can pick up our words and mimic them, but do not understand what they are saying.

Shrimp in concert

Shrimp and other animals that swarm at the sea surface make constant clicking sounds, which we can hear if we lower a microphone into the water. We do not know how they do it or why, but several million shrimp clicking together in concert make a crackling roar, which could help keep predatory fish away.

Growling and roaring

A lion's roar starts as a deep-throated growl. You need to be nearby to hear the growl, but the roar carries for miles on a still evening. It is mainly large males that roar, usually those in charge of a pride – a group of females and young. It sounds angry, but it is just a warning to other male lions to keep away.

Don't lions roar all the time? No, the lions, lionesses, and cubs talk to each other mostly in quiet, low-pitched growls.

Rubbing legs

Crickets are grasshopper-like insects that live in warm tropical regions. Often they live in houses, where they emerge in the evenings to chirrup noisily. They make the sound by rubbing together the long joints of their hind legs. Only the males chirrup, mostly after the heat of the day, in an effort to attract mates.

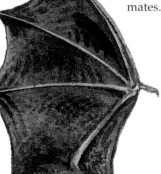

Echo-location

Pipistrelles – small, dark brown bats with black wings – emerge from caves and house lofts on warm summer evenings. As they fly, they emit high-pitched squeaks, which echo from trees, walls, wires, and flying insects. The returning echoes help the bats avoid obstacles in the half light and identify and catch their evening meal of insects. Young people may hear the squeaks, but older people often lose their ability to detect such high notes.

Hearing in water

Songs across the seas

Humpback whales live in all the world's oceans. They migrate toward polar waters for food in summer, and back to the warm equatorial waters in winter. Their songs travel dozens of miles under water.

Warbling seals

Weddell seals emit high-pitched warbling calls that come back to them as echoes if there are fish in the water nearby.

Do whales sing to one another? Whales, and their smaller cousins the dolphins and porpoises, make a surprising amount of noise in the water. We can sometimes hear part of it on a still evening when the sea is calm. But the best way is to lower a hydrophone (that's a special kind of microphone) into the water. Then we hear all kinds of squeaks, groans, burps, chirps, crackles, and – yes – long, wavering musical notes just like singing. Whales use these different kinds of sounds for different purposes. Humpback whales particularly have musical voices.

Smacking the water

Another way of making sounds is to hit the water hard with flippers or tail, or leap out and fall back with a smack. These sounds also travel miles, telling other whales something is happening. Often they are made by a male to attract females.

Males sing loud and long when they are about to set off on their long migrations – as though they are telling each other it's time to go, and maybe to keep in touch while they are traveling. They sing during the mating season, repeating phrases over and over just as we do, and singing a slightly different song each year. Why? We can only guess.

Clicking dolphins

Dolphins are especially good at echo-location. These bottlenose dolphins, hunting in the dark, are sending out high-pitched clicking sounds. The sounds bounce off prey and are echoed back. From the return signals the dolphins can tell where the fish are, how big, how many, and even what kind.

Vibrations

Ground vibrations
Though earthworms have no eyes, they respond to light. Similarly, they have no special organs for hearing, but are alerted by vibrations through the ground. Earthworms lying half-out on

Sound waves are vibrations within ranges of frequency that an animal's ears – like ours – can detect and analyze. Do some animals hear things that we can't? Yes, animals such as dogs and cats can pick up higher frequencies than humans. At lower frequencies, rather than hear vibrations, we feel them as rumbles and shaking. These, too, can be useful in telling us about the world. They can be early warnings, and different kinds of animals use them in different ways.

These nestling sparrows (opposite page), less than three days old, were blind and deaf on hatching, and are still too young to see or hear their parents. However, they can feel and respond to vibrations. When a parent returns with food and shakes the nest on landing, up shoot the three hungry bills, gaping to be fed. Juvenile fleas, web-building spiders, ant-lions, and earthworms all make use of vibrations at different stages in their lives.

Keeping in touch
This spider sits with one leg touching its newly spun web. A fly entangled in any part of the web sets up vibrations that the spider immediately feels. In seconds it runs over and captures the fly.

the surface will often withdraw into their burrows when other animals pass close by – a useful response when so many animals eat them. The slight ground vibration is enough to alert them, setting up the same safety response as a sudden bright light.

Opposite page: As soon as they feel a parent returning to the nest, these nestling sparrows are up and ready for food.

Jumping fleas
A flea's eggs hatch into tiny maggots, which become pupae. Inside each pupa a new flea develops. A slight shaking, caused by a passing animal, is all the new flea needs. It jumps out, ready to climb onto the passer-by.

Setting a trap
Ant-lions are the larvae, or immature forms, of delicate long-winged flies. So-called because of their strength and ferocity, they live in sandy soils, each in a conical pit, where it waits, half-covered in sand. An insect falling into the pit causes vibrations that alert the ant-lion, which jumps out and grabs and kills it.

Feeling warmth

Most bats eat insects that they catch on the wing. Vampires are small bats that specialize in taking blood from warm-blooded animals.

Keeping young warm

All kinds of warm-blooded animals give birth to young that, for their first few days or weeks, cannot keep themselves warm enough. Many birds sit with their small chicks, and many mammals such as cats (above) stay close to their young, warming them with their own bodies. When looking after young birds or mammals that have lost their parents, it is important to keep them warm.

Do some animals warm up in the morning sun? Mammals, including ourselves, are warm-blooded. That means that our bodies run at a high and constant temperature, around 98°-99°F (37°C). Our bodies maintain this temperature automatically when we use our muscles and eat the right kinds of food.

Birds, too, are warm-blooded, while insects, fish, and reptiles are cold-blooded. But most cold-blooded animals work better when they are warm. That is why snakes and lizards like to warm up in the sun on a cold morning.

We have sensors that tell us if we are too warm or too cold, and our skin can detect warmth outside. The South American vampire bat likes to drink warm blood. Hunting in the late evening, and using the heat sensors on its face, it finds a cow, and makes a small nick in the skin of the heel with its sharp front teeth. Now it licks the blood that flows from the wound.

Blood-sucking leech

Leeches feed by sucking the blood of different kinds of warm-blooded animals. How do they find them? Some that live in tropical forests are heat-sensitive. They climb to the tips of low-growing tree branches, and drop when they sense a warm-blooded animal passing underneath.

Seeking warmth

Snakes have sensory organs that help them find warm places. On a chill night in the Arizona desert, this rattlesnake has found a sleeping camper, and is about to curl up with him in his sleeping bag. The camper is the warmest object for miles around. It is a good reason never to sleep on the ground when snakes are around.

Seeking a host

The size of a pinhead, lice are blood-sucking insects that were once very common, especially among poor people. Today we see very few. They are found in brickwork, between floorboards, in furniture, and in clothing, and live by biting humans and sucking their blood. Lice can remain inactive for several months on end. When they need a meal, they come out from hiding and look for a host, attracted by the warmth of the human body.

Touching and feeling

Tentacles

Sea anemones have sensitive touch receptors on all their tentacles. When another animal touches any of them, messages pass through a network of nerves, and all the tentacles come together to trap and hold the prey.

Whiskers

Cats have long whiskers that grow from fleshy pads on either side of their upper lip, well supplied with sensory nerves. Hunting by night, domestic cats use their whiskers to sense where they are going, whether they can squeeze through small gaps as well as picking up the vibrations of nearby prey.

Some animals depend for a living mainly on the sense of touch. Like most animals, we have receptors all over our skin, with concentrations in special places that need to be particularly sensitive, such as our fingers. But are fingers necessary for a good sense of touch? Some animals use other parts of their body for feeling.

This walrus, living in cold Arctic seas, has a particularly tough and insensitive hide. Its most sensitive areas are the roots of the bristles on either side of the upper lip. Why does it need them? Because it feeds on clams, which it finds by raking with its tusks through muddy seabeds. The water is too muddy for it to see the clams, but it feels them with its sensitive bristles and takes them into its mouth.

The other animals on these pages have touch receptors concentrated in different places, but mostly on the front, or head – the part that meets the world first – including other important sensory organs such as eyes, ears, noses, and tongues.

Right: Walruses need a tough hide to survive in cold Arctic seas, but use their sensitive bristles to find food in muddy waters.

Feelers

Encased in a hard, jointed shell, the crayfish probably feels very little through most of its surface. By contrast, its long, many-jointed antennae, or feelers, are extremely sensitive, whisking constantly through the water and over the ground ahead and to either side.

Barbels

Catfish are so called because the long fleshy spikes – called antennae, or barbels – that surround their mouth reminded fishermen of cats' whiskers. Just like whiskers, they are well supplied with nerves. Catfish often live in muddy rivers. As they move forward in the water, they use the barbels to sweep the water and ground ahead of them and immediately underneath, feeling for prey and anything else of interest.

Special sensors

Skin sensors

Most whales and dolphins are smooth and streamlined. Humpback whales are covered with knobs, especially on their face and the leading edge of their huge flippers. What are the bumps for? They might be skin sensors that tell the whales when they are passing through shoals of small fish and crustaceans on which they feed.

This duck-billed platypus lives in Tasmania, off southern Australia, and hunts in a greeny-brown world along the bed of a small river. Worms and insect larvae are its main foods. The river is often too murky for it to see clearly, but the soft skin covering its bill-like nose is very sensitive to touch, much more so than the rest of its fur-covered body. So it digs its bill into the green weed and mud, snapping when it makes contact with something that feels like food.

Are some animals more sensitive to touch than we are? Some have special touch receptors for different purposes. The knobs and bumps covering a humpback whale might have something to do with its feeding on small floating animals. The accuracy of albatross flight might depend on touch receptors in its wing tips. Shoaling fish probably receive signals from each other through sensitive skin receptors. And touch receptors in their skin help to protect many animals from surface parasites, telling them when to scratch.

Left: The soft, greeny-gray skin covering the bill is sensitive to touch, helping the platypus find worms and insects in the stream bed.

Synchronized swimming

Fish that swim in shoals, sometimes many thousands, twist and turn at exactly the same time. We do not know how they manage this, but each fish feels the presence and movements of its neighbors through sensitive skin receptors on its sides.

Wing-tip sensors

How does an albatross skim so low over the sea, with wing tips almost but not quite touching the water? Some scientists think they have sensors in the bases of the wing-tip feathers that respond to small pressure changes, telling the albatross when the tip of the feather is very close to the sea.

Itching and scratching

All animals need sensitive skin to warn them of parasites – fleas, lice, ticks, mosquitoes, leeches, and other pests that damage the skin or suck blood. A slight itch somewhere near its neck has set this dog scratching, a reflex (automatic reaction) that might get rid of whatever is causing the itch.

Mother and baby elephant see and smell each other, but seem more content if they can touch each other as well.

Close together

Bunching up

Born blind and helpless, wolf cubs grow quickly. At five or six weeks they play-fight and roll together in their den. If a fox or other stranger appears, the cubs bunch up tightly, snarling and showing their teeth. Once they have left the den, they separate and are never again quite so close.

Humans are a sociable species and mostly enjoy the company of friends or relatives. We often demonstrate this by means of touch – as in shaking hands, hugging, or kissing. Are some animals like us in this respect? Touching is particularly important to baby animals of some species. This young elephant, just a few weeks old, walks every day with the herd, usually keeping very close to mother. It wanders off from time to time, but always finds her again, recognizing her by sight and scent, and trots just in front of her. She can see and smell it, but she touches it gently, too, with the tip of her trunk – a reassurance for both of them.

Other mammals and birds show similar responses. Wolf cubs bundle closely together if danger threatens their den. Young grebes climb aboard their parents, nestling close among their feathers, and young penguins huddle close while their parents are away at sea. Earwigs and some other invertebrate animals also settle together, gaining something important from the close skin contact.

Taking a ride

Within hours of hatching from the eggs, grebe chicks leave their floating nest and take to the water. It will be weeks before they can fly, but they can float, swim, and dive, paddling

after their parents in search of food. At night they climb aboard the parents, snuggling down among the feathers of the back, where they are warm, comfortable, and safe from predators.

In a huddle

Insects and other invertebrates often huddle together, especially during winter when it is too cold for them to live actively. Finding corners where the temperature and humidity (dampness) are right, these earwigs pack together for several weeks in close contact.

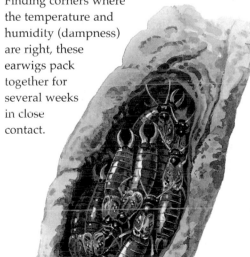

In a huddle 2

These adelie penguin chicks stay in their nest with one parent while the other parent hunts for food at sea. After two to three weeks, both parents go hunting, so the chicks from neighboring nests huddle tightly together for warmth and mutual protection.

Smell and taste

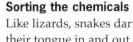

Tasting or smelling?

Lizards and snakes live close to the ground, where scents in the air and along trails are easily confused. While moving, their long tongues flick constantly in and out, sampling the air around and the ground beneath them. Is this tasting or smelling?

Beaded lizard

Smell is the ability to detect and recognize very small concentrations of chemicals in the air around us. We do it by absorbing the chemicals on the damp surface inside our noses. Simpler animals absorb them through their skin. Taste buds, which contain taste receptors, are grouped on the tongue and other parts of the mouth. They send information about the chemicals in the food to the brain. Smell and taste are very closely bound together.

Do some animals rely more on their sense of smell than we do? We value our sense of smell, but it is nowhere near as sensitive as that of other animals, nor do we use it in so many ways. Rescue dogs (right), trained by alpine guides, use their sensitive noses to sniff out humans under several feet of snow. Vultures, lizards, snakes, and butterflies all use similar senses in their daily lives.

Sorting the chemicals

Like lizards, snakes dart their tongue in and out, then curl it back into the roof of their mouth to touch a pit-shaped patch of sensory cells called the Jacobson's organ. This sorts the chemicals that the tongue brought in from the air and ground, alerting the reptile to food or danger. Similarly, our own tongue and nose often act together, blending our senses of taste and smell.

Responding to scents

Butterflies have a great sense of smell, and respond to scents from flowers that tell them when nectar is flowing. They may also be attracted by scent to mates. Males sometimes travel long distances to find a female ready for mating. The scent organs of this clouded yellow butterfly are located mainly on its antennae and legs.

Sniffing the air

Most birds seem to have very little sense of smell. But some sea birds that live on oily fish and plankton (small drifting animals), and land birds that live on carrion (dead animals) are exceptions. Turkey vultures, or buzzards, of North and South America soar on updrafts, sniffing the air for the telltale smell of a dead or rotting carcass.

Avalanches in alpine regions sometimes result in skiers being buried under several feet of snow. Trained rescue dogs use their acute sense of smell to find them.

Wild scents

Following a trail
Wood ants travel the forest floor, picking up tiny twigs and seeds to take back to their nests. Often you see them following each other, or at least following trails that they seem to know about but you cannot see. Do they have a special sense? No, these trails are marked by a scent given off in tiny amounts by the ants themselves. They just follow it back home.

One useful thing about scents as messengers is that a very little goes a long way. A tiny amount of scented material can travel on the air, to be picked up several miles away. Even smaller amounts can be spread along a trail, to be detected and interpreted days or weeks later. Large amounts can be quite overpowering.

Are scents always used to attract? This North American skunk produces a foul-smelling oily material in glands close to its tail. If threatened, it can shoot the scented fluid a few feet. The scent sticks to whatever it touches, and can last for weeks. Most predators avoid skunks.

Other animals use scents for other purposes. Ants follow the minutely marked trails left by other ants. Hoverflies seek the scents of particular flowers. And the females of many animals give off particular scents when they are ready to mate.

Attracting a mate
The female husky dog (below left) is "on heat," her ovaries having produced eggs. If she mates now, she is likely to have puppies. She gives off a scent that travels in the air, sometimes for several miles, attracting male dogs to her.

Finding nectar
Like many other insects, hoverflies are attracted to flowers, from which they can draw nectar, a sugary syrup that gives them energy. The main attraction is scent, which tells them in which direction the flowers lie. Having found the flowers, they are attracted by color as well. Color helps them identify particular kinds of flowers that produce the nectar they want.

Alarmed by an approaching predator, this skunk has raised its hind end and is ready to release a foul-smelling fluid.

Electric fields

Radar screen

Mormyrid fish live in African freshwater streams and lakes, feeding on insects and worms they dig out of the mud. There are many species, and all can generate electric fields like radar screens around themselves. When they cannot see in muddy water, their radar tells them of other fish or obstacles nearby.

Electric hunter

A dogfish hunting over a sandy seabed may stop and dig out a flounder or other small fish. How does it know the fish is there? Dogfish are thought to hunt mainly by scent, but at close quarters like this they use another sense – electricity. The very small breathing movements of the flounder generate tiny electrical impulses that the dogfish can detect through its skin.

Left: This electric eel generates and discharges small amounts of electricity to find its way around, and much larger amounts to stun frogs and other fish.

Can some fish give electric shocks? All animals, including humans, generate small electric charges in their muscles. Several kinds of fish have developed special muscular organs that work like batteries, producing electricity and channeling it for special use in their daily lives. This electric eel from the Amazon River, about 6.5 feet (2 m) long, has three "batteries" that together amount to half its weight. It can give a strong electric shock – the kind you would get from a live electric wire – if you touch it or even swim close to it. The blue electric ray gives smaller shocks. Other kinds of fish develop an electric field around them, like a radar screen. It does not harm other fish that come within the field – they do not even feel it – but it gives advance warning when something is approaching. Dogfish and sharks, which are closely related, generate little or no electricity themselves, but are sensitive to the electric fields of other fish.

Dogfish

Electric ray

Sensory skin

A shark's head is covered with lines of tiny pits called ampullae, which are sensitive to tiny electric currents. What are they for? Possibly to detect prey; and perhaps to tell the shark which way the ocean current is flowing. This would help the shark detect the earth's magnetic field, and find its way around.

Powerful batteries

Rays are flat fish that live on the seabed. Several kinds generate small amounts of electricity to screen the water around them. Electric rays have powerful batteries at the base of their front fins that generate up to 200 volts. They direct a charge of electricity toward another fish, stunning it so that it cannot swim away.

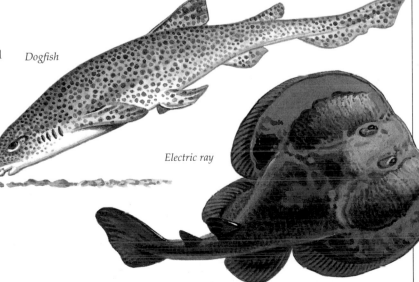

Which way is up?

Defying gravity
If gravity pulls everything down, how do birds fly? Swimmers stay up by pushing water downward. Similarly, birds stay up by pushing air downward. Heavy birds like swans and geese push a lot of air

down with each flapping wingbeat. Lighter ones like these swifts have smaller, but faster wingbeats. Flight requires birds to have much more delicate senses of gravity and balance than mammals, with finer muscular control and coordination of movement.

Do animals know which way is up? We do, because we are so used to gravity – the force that pulls us toward the ground – that we often forget about it. Astronauts in space learn what it is like to be without gravity and not to know which way is up. They are weightless – there is nothing to hold them or anything else to the ground. Animals that live in water have a similar experience, because they too are almost weightless – the water supports them. Some rely on light to tell "above" from "below" – light usually comes from above. Others have special sensory organs that tell them when they are upside-down.

Mammals and birds usually like to be right side up. Our blood circulation and digestive systems work better that way. On the other hand, three-toed sloths of South America spend virtually their whole lives hanging upside-down from branches in the dense rainforest. Their long spindly arms and legs are the wrong shape for standing upright on the ground.

Sloths move slowly from tree to tree, hanging below the branches and feeding on leaves and shoots. They would find it much more difficult to walk on the forest floor below, which is often waterlogged or flooded.

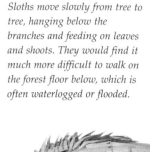

Staying upright
Jellyfish move through the water by "pulsating." Waves of contraction pass down from the top of the bell to the edges, forcing the water out and the jellyfish upward. If strong currents topple the jellyfish onto its side, tiny sensors along the rim of the bell tell it what has happened, and the waves of contraction alter to turn it the right side up.

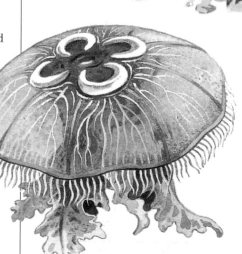

When up is down
Turn a lobster on its back and, like most other animals, it will turn a somersault to end the right side up. How does it know? First, by seeing where the light comes from – light usually comes from above, so that is "up." Then, it has statocysts – tiny cells at the base of its antennae that tell it which direction is down. Shine a light from below, and it might decide "up" is "down" and turn over.

Under pressure

The pearly nautilus lives in a spiral shell that contains a bubble of air. It rises by adding more air to the bubble. To feed, it leans from its shell and shoots out tentacles that grasp passing fish and plankton.

We notice atmospheric pressure – the weight of air constantly pressing down on us – even less than gravity. Some people and animals seem sensitive to atmospheric pressure changes. We do not know how birds or mammals sense them. Animals with a gas or air bladder, such as the salmon or the nautilus, probably sense changes in the volume of the bladder.

The pearly nautilus (left) lives in shallow tropical seas. During the day it lives on the seabed, held down by its shell. At night it releases gases into its shell and rises toward the surface.

Water also exerts pressure, which increases very quickly with depth. How is it that some animals can adapt to changes in pressure when we can't? Even with diving equipment, human divers find it hard to work below about 300 feet (100 m), but seals and some whales can dive to much greater depths.

Displacing water
Related to snails, octopus, and squid, cuttlefish live on the sea floor, where they hunt actively for crabs and other small animals. They travel by emitting jets of water. A porous, chalky shell or bone inside them acts as a variable gas chamber. When the shell is filled with water, its weight holds the cuttlefish down. When the water is displaced with gases released from the blood, the cuttlefish floats over the seabed.

Pressure at depth
Water is heavy, and pressure increases rapidly with depth. Yet sperm whales and some other species of toothed whales can descend to 3,000 feet (1,000 m) and more, and remain below for several hours at a time. They take very little air down with them, though plenty of oxygen dissolved in their blood. And their bodies are built to tolerate the enormous pressures at those depths.

Why fish don't sink
Like many other fish, salmon are slightly denser than the water they live in. They are kept from sinking by their air sac, a bladder of gas close to their backbone. They can add to the amount of gas in the bladder or take some away. So they float at the right depth in the water with only small movements of muscles and fins.

Above: This cutaway drawing of a salmon shows the gas bladder that fish use to prevent them from sinking.

Changing color

Now you see me ...
Soft-bodied mollusks related to squid, cuttlefish, and snails, octopi have a squat, round body and a mantle of eight legs, each lined with one or two rows of suckers. The biggest ones span up to 10 feet (3 m), but most are much smaller. They crawl on the seabed, searching with two large, well-developed eyes for clams, crabs, and fish.

Their skin color changes rapidly, making them almost invisible against sandy, muddy, or pebble backgrounds.

Changing the spots
Several kinds of bottom-living fish alter shape during their first weeks of life, changing from round-bodied to flat. As adults they lie flat on the sea floor, swimming by undulating their bodies and fins. Like this plaice, nearly all can change color, altering the size and color of their spots to match the background on which they are lying.

Here is a green lizard called a chameleon, sitting very still among green leaves on an African forest tree. If you were not looking closely, you might not see it at all. Neither would the insects that the chameleon is stalking, nor the predators that might like a fat chameleon for breakfast. It is a good example of camouflage – an animal closely matching its background.

But can a chameleon change color? Yes – if it climbed onto a different kind of tree with reddish leaves, it would turn reddish to match its new background. In strong sunlight it would be brighter, in the evening duller, and at night dark brown. These changes are made automatically through complex layers of color cells in its skin that alter according to the surface and the intensity of light. An octopus and plaice can change color as they move. Peppered moths come in different colors, but cannot change from one to another.

Chameleons move very slowly and deliberately. Their eyes swivel independently, and they can throw out a tongue almost as long as their body to catch flies and other insects at a distance.

Matching backgrounds
This peppered moth, spanning 2 inches (5 cm) across the wings, appears in a range of shades from completely black to almost pure white. Peppered moths rest during the day on tree trunks, where predatory birds find and eat them. Dark moths were rare up to a century ago, but are now more common, particularly in cities and industrial areas. Why? Because hunting birds find dark moths harder to spot on tree trunks dirty with soot.

Index